CW01652751

Best wishes,

Pamela S. Sykes.

THE BROWNIES THROW A PARTY

PAMELA SYKES

The Brownies throw a party

ILLUSTRATED BY
JANINA EDE

HODDER AND STOUGHTON
LONDON SYDNEY AUCKLAND TORONTO

For Jane Longbourne

ISBN 0 340 19970 9

First published 1976
Third impression 1987

Published by Hodder and Stoughton Children's Books,
a division of Hodder and Stoughton Ltd,
Mill Road, Dunton Green, Sevenoaks, Kent TN13 2YJ

Printed in Great Britain by T. J. Press (Padstow) Ltd,
Padstow, Cornwall

Contents

1 *The lost children*

'Spring,' announced Tracey, looking round the park with approval, 'is definitely here at last!'

It certainly was. A late afternoon sun slanted across blossomy trees and glowing flower-beds.

'Even the grass feels bouncy,' Jane agreed, bouncing a few steps to prove it.

'And everybody's looking cheerful,' Susan pointed out. 'That's always a sign that winter's over.'

Tracey turned a cartwheel. 'I couldn't do that this time last year,' she said with satisfaction.

'Are you sure you ought to now?' Jane asked a little anxiously. Tracey had broken her leg the summer before.

'Absolutely sure. Dr Martin said it's as good as new now. Perhaps better, because bones heal up very strongly.' Tracey did another cartwheel. It went rather wrong and she landed in a heap on the grass. 'Bother!' she exclaimed. 'I need a bit more practice.'

'*More* practice!' said Susan. 'You never stop!'

'She can't help it,' said Jane, who had been Tracey's best friend for years. 'She's always been like that. That's why she's got her Agility Interest badge, and Athlete, and Swimmer —'

'— and I'm working for my Cyclist,' Tracey put in. 'But,' she added, to make things fair, 'I couldn't possibly do the badges Jane has – Animal Lover, and Needlework and Writer, and Book Lover, and Knitter —'

'Goodness!' cried Susan. 'Shall I *ever* catch up?'

'Probably not,' Jane told her. 'And it doesn't matter a bit. Interest badges are fun, but not so very important. And after all, you've only been a Brownie a little time.' Jane was anxious to make Susan feel at home in the newly-formed Six, the Elves, of which she herself had been made Sixer.

At first Tracey had found it difficult to get used to this. For a long time she had been the one to tell Jane what to do, and Jane had happily done it. Now things were different. Tracey tried not to mind. But sometimes, secretly, she did.

Another thing that was hard to bear was that Jane and Susan had made friends so easily and quickly. Tracey tried not to feel left out, but sometimes – this afternoon, for instance – it was a little difficult.

She turned another cartwheel to cheer herself up.

The other two were discussing whether Susan was ready to take her House Orderly badge.

'The worst bit is seeing the smears on the window when you think you've finished,' Susan was saying.

'My Mum says washing-up liquid is the best thing,' Jane advised. 'Gran uses vinegar-and-water and an old newspaper, though —'

Tracey felt this housewifey conversation was all wrong for such an out-of-doors day.

'Let's forget about badges and do something more interesting,' she suggested.

The others seemed not to hear her.

'Of course you *can* clean a basin or a cupboard instead of a window,' Jane said.

'Dull,' said Susan.

'They're all dull jobs in the house,' said Tracey

firmly. 'Forget them. If I were you, Susan, I'd —'

'But I want to have a go at this one, Trace, and Jane says —'

'Jane doesn't know everything.'

'But she is my Sixer.'

Oh, bother them, thought Tracey. She stood on her hands again, and took four paces. Better. Let them get on with their dull gossip. She didn't care. And Jane must be a boring Sixer, encouraging people to go in for badges like that. All the same, she was trying to think of something disagreeable to say when suddenly all conversation was made impossible.

With a loud chorus of yells, about eight girls and boys, all older than the Brownies, came swooping along on roller skates. Down the broad path they raced, their skates making a loud rattle on the hard surface. As they shouted, they elbowed and jostled each other for first place. They behaved as if they were the only people in the park. The Brownies might just as well have not been on the path, for all the notice the skaters took of them. Grind – rattle – yell – the big boys and girls swept towards them.

Tracey was already on the grass, but the other two had to skip quickly out of the way.

'Look here —' shouted Tracey indignantly as a flying skate nearly caught her leg.

Scornful boos and whistles were the only answer. Already the race was past them, pursuing its noisy way round the park.

Jane stared after them. 'Just think if we'd been *old* people we couldn't have got out of their way. Rude beasts.'

'I'd like to tell them what I think of them,' said Tracey, her face pink. 'If they come round again,' she added threateningly, 'I will —'

'So will I,' Jane promised loyally, though afraid of the big rough children.

'Oh don't – *please* don't!' begged Susan, looking so agitated that the others stared at her.

'But they've got no right —' Jane began.

'*Somebody*'s got to tell them,' said Tracey fiercely.

'But not us, not us,' said Susan, almost tearfully. 'You don't know them.'

'Do you?' Jane asked curiously.

'No. Yes. In a way. They're a Gang. Bill, my big

brother used to belong to them, but not any more. When Trevor – that was the big one in front – made himself head, they – they – well, they're not the kind of Gang to belong to now.'

'I'll believe *that*,' said Tracey. 'What else do they do?'

Susan seemed unwilling to explain. Jane could see how nearly she was to crying. 'Never mind, Susan,' – she made a quick face at Tracey – 'You can tell us another day. I think it's time we were getting home for tea.'

This seemed a good idea. Somehow some of the brightness had gone out of the afternoon. This was only partly because the Gang had spoiled things. It was also because the sun was setting, and the air had a chill.

'Brrr!' Jane buttoned up her cardigan.

'You should take more exercise, like me,' said Tracey, turning a last cartwheel to prove her point.

All the same it was getting colder. And Susan looked really shivery. Perhaps they had better be getting along.

Other people were drifting out of the park towards

the warmth of their homes. Although Susan several times looked fearfully over her shoulder, the Gang, too, had disappeared.

'Any minute now there'll be only birds left,' remarked Jane, 'having a terrific last-minute scavenge for their families' suppers.'

But here she was wrong, for round the very next corner they stopped at the same moment to listen.

'What is it?' Susan asked, eyes wide. 'An animal?'

Tracey shook her head. 'Somebody crying. Somebody very small.'

'Behind those bushes,' whispered Jane, nodding towards a clump of laurels.

They looked at each other. Then together they tiptoed towards the sound.

Behind the bushes they found two tiny boys with coffee-coloured skin, sleek black hair and enormous eyes from which large tears were rolling fast. The smaller of the two – who surely could not have been more than three years old – was making the little whimpers they had heard. The elder brother held his hand tightly.

'Hello,' said Jane. 'Where's Mummy?'

The little boys merely opened their eyes even wider and said nothing. The elder one sniffed.

'Are you lost?' Tracey asked.

No answer.

It was difficult to know if the little boys could not understand, or were too shy to answer. The little one cried harder.

'Here – don't,' Tracey urged. 'You're not lost now. You're found. We've found you. Where do you live?'

But their questions received no replies.

'Well there's *one* thing we can do anyway,' said Jane firmly. She produced a clean handkerchief and mopped up both wet little faces. 'There now, that's better isn't it?' she added in an encouraging voice.

More tears fell.

'Oh dear,' said Susan. 'We must do something. Look how cold they are. They haven't half enough on.' Indeed the boys wore only their shirts and jeans.

Jane took off her own cardigan and wrapped it round the smallest. Tracey did the same for his brother before Susan had time to. 'They can't stay out here, that's for sure. It'll be dark soon.'

'We'd better take them home,' said Susan.

'No,' Tracey and Jane disagreed together.

'Somebody'll be worrying like anything,' Jane pointed out.

'The proper thing to do is take them to the Police Station,' said Tracey.

'The police!' exclaimed Susan. 'Oh, *no*. Let's keep clear of them.'

Jane was puzzled. 'But Tracey's absolutely right. We ought to have thought of that at once.'

'The sooner the better,' Tracey began to take charge as usual. 'Come along,' she ordered the little boys. 'We're going to find Mummy. Well, we are,' she added in a lower tone to Jane. 'In the end.'

'Not me,' said Susan. 'I'm not going to the Police Station.'

'But why not?' Jane wanted to know.

'My Mum wants me home for tea early,' said Susan. 'I must get a move on, I'm late already. Cheerio. See you tomorrow.' She hurried away.

'Well, what's up with her?' Tracey demanded.

Jane frowned. Clearly Susan was afraid of the police for some reason. Some reason that must be looked into. But not now. There was a more important matter to be dealt with. She put her arm round the smallest boy. 'Come on,' she said kindly.

But clearly the brothers, though willing to be taken charge of, were too tired to walk far.

'I know. Pick-a-back,' said Tracey. She hoisted the elder brother on to her back. Jane took the younger. Soon tears changed to chuckles, as the little party set off through the gently falling dusk.

2 *Police to the rescue*

The Brownies carefully lowered their burdens to the ground, but tightly held their hands.

Jane doubtfully looked at the large doorway. 'Do we just go in?'

'I don't know,' Tracey admitted. It was one thing to talk of visiting a Police Station, but another actually to enter, she discovered. 'There isn't a notice saying "Please Ring", or anything.'

'Nor one saying "Please Walk In",' Jane pointed out.

'But we will, all the same,' said Tracey, and before she could lose her courage, turned the big handle of the door, opened it, and went boldly inside.

Jane followed.

Almost at once there was another door with a glass

panel in it. They peered through this. Beyond was a bare room, a long counter, a policeman standing behind it.

'Just like on television,' whispered Jane. She prodded Tracey from behind. 'Go on.'

'All very well for you —' Tracey began – but there was nothing else she could do but obey.

As they entered, the policeman who had been making a list, looked up.

'Well?' he said, but kindly. 'What can I do for you?'

'We thought we'd better come —' Tracey began, and faltered.

'Because of Lost and Found things. You know, you're supposed to report them, aren't you?' said Tracey.

'True enough,' agreed the policeman. 'Have you lost something or found something?'

'Found,' said Tracey. 'But not something, some-*body* – two bodies, well, not *bodies* exactly —'

'Shall we begin again at the beginning?' suggested the policeman.

'Yes, do let's,' said Jane, feeling that Brownies

should be dealing with this situation much better than they were. 'We two – that's Tracey and me, have found these two little boys in the park.'

The small children, feeling that they were being talked about, gazed up at the policeman.

'Ah, now we're getting somewhere,' he said, opening a large book. 'First of all, let's have your full names and addresses, shall we?'

This information at least they were able to pass on exactly and sensibly. Then they explained exactly how they had found the boys cold and crying behind the bushes.

'You did quite the right thing to bring them here,' said the policeman. 'We'll soon have them at home again. Now then what are *their* names?'

'We don't know,' said Tracey.

'They don't seem to know themselves,' said Jane.

The policeman leaned over the counter. 'What – are – your – names?'

The little boys glanced at each other then back at the policeman without a word.

'Hmm,' he said. 'What we need is a W. P. C.'

'A what?' exclaimed Jane, slightly alarmed.

'A Woman Police Constable. They're better at this kind of problem than I am.' He spoke briefly into the telephone on the counter, and in a minute or two a young woman in uniform appeared. She smiled at the Brownies. 'Hello, I'm Police Constable Randle, and—'

The door burst open and a very angry man strode up to the counter and began to bellow at the policeman. 'Look here, this is the third time I've had to come and complain—'

'Just a minute please, sir. I'm attending to another matter,' said the policeman calmly. He turned to Constable Randle. 'Take this little party into the Interview Room would you, and see if you can get them sorted out? And while you're at it—'

'I'm not prepared to hang about while a parcel of kids—' blustered the complaining man.

'—I think there are some chocolate biscuits around somewhere,' the policeman went on as if there had been no interruption.

Constable Randle winked at the Brownies and beckoned them to follow her. As they walked down a passage the loud angry voice of the complaining man could still be heard on the subject of cars being parked across the entrance to his drive.

'Are there many people like that?' Jane asked Constable Randle.

'Oh, we get all kinds in here,' she answered cheerfully. 'The Duty Sergeant has to put up with worse than that sometimes.' She led them into a small warm room containing only a square table and several hard chairs. 'This isn't very grand, but we'll soon fix ourselves up.'

She turned out to be a very good fixer up. In no time she had found two grey blankets to wrap warmly round the boys so that the Brownies could have their cardigans back. She said hot drinks and biscuits were on the way, and meanwhile would anyone be worrying about the girls at home? Jane and Tracey thought their mothers might get anxious soon, neither was allowed out after dusk – and when she learned they were not on the telephone the constable said she would have messages sent by car.

'Thank you,' said Tracey. 'That's very kind. Only —' she stopped.

'Only —?'

Tracey looked at Jane who knew exactly what she was thinking.

'You see,' Jane explained to the constable, 'last time a policeman suddenly called on Tracey's Mum it was to tell her Tracey had had an accident. So this time, she'll have an awful shock all over again when she sees the uniform.' She felt ungrateful as she spoke, but Constable Randle seemed to understand at once. 'Then we won't make it a Panda car and we'll cover up the uniform this time. Don't worry, I said I was a good fixer.' She vanished.

'They do take trouble, don't they?' said Tracey. 'It's a pity Susan isn't here to see how kind they are.'

'Yes it is,' Jane agreed thoughtfully.

'Do you know what *I* think?' asked Tracey.

'Yes I do, and I think you're wrong. I don't think she's been in trouble, but I think her brother might have.'

'The one that was with the Gang?'

'Yes.'

'Then I expect he deserved the trouble. But there's no need for poor Susan to be afraid of the police just because of that. Brown Owl wouldn't think that was right. I'll have a talk with Susan and —'

'I'll have a talk with Susan,' Jane said quietly.

'Now look here—' began Tracey with energy. She felt the bright little eyes of their eldest 'find' fixed apprehensively on her. She decided to keep her words for Jane until later.

Constable Randle reappeared with a tray of hot tea, lemonade and chocolate biscuits. Soon everyone was eating and drinking.

Constable Randle smiled round at the small gathering. She pointed to herself. 'Me, Mary Randle.' Then to the Brownies in turn. 'Jane', 'Tracey'. She pointed at the eldest little boy. 'You—?' But he did not respond, though he appeared to understand the point of her game. Instead he grinned, and took another biscuit.

The constable sighed. 'Well, I don't know. No children have been reported missing yet.' She looked at her watch. 'You'd think that by now —'

There was a tremendous flurry of voices from outside the room. The little boys sat up straight, their eyes suddenly on the door. It opened. In swept a dark-skinned woman, with shiny black hair. She rushed up to the boys, grabbing them to her as if she hadn't seen them for a year at least. It was difficult to tell from her shrill flow of foreign words if she was more angry or excited. But you could tell how she was relieved to be with her children again.

In the doorway a dark girl of about Tracey's age stood uncertainly. Her mother turned to her accusingly. The girl answered back. There was a rapid conversation in their own language. It seemed as if the mother was reproachful, the daughter excusing herself.

Finally, the little girl turned to the Brownies, smiling shyly but speaking in English. 'There was a mistake. My mother was shopping. I was playing with friends. I thought the boys were with her. She thought they were with me. So both of us thought they were safe. All the time the naughty little things had run across the road – just think of all those cars – all the way to the park. We hardly ever have time to take them there. We're so glad they're found. My mother says she wants to thank you a thousand times.'

This the mother then proceeded to do in her own

language. It was rather embarrassing being thanked a thousand times. Much talk followed, the little girl translating when necessary. They learned her name was Farida. Her little brothers were Mumtas and Behal. The family name was Mirza. They had come from Pakistan. It was rather muddling, but Police Constable Randle was all smiles. The official records were put straight. Mrs Mirza – if that was the proper thing to call her – put on the boys' own little jackets she had hopefully brought with her. Everyone said goodbye to everyone else. Then Farida said, 'We'd all be awfully pleased if you'd come and have tea with us at our home?'

Of course Tracey and Jane were glad to accept, though they said they would have to make it right with their mothers first. They made a note of the address: 'Belleview Mansions'. It sounded very grand.

Then – most exciting of all – two police cars arrived – the Mirza family was driven home in one direction. Tracey and Jane in the other. It was fun to draw up at Jane's house and see people stare curiously at them.

'I'm rather sorry the adventure has ended,' Tracey admitted.

'Me too,' agreed Jane, as she got out.

What neither of them knew was that a brand-new adventure had just begun!

3 *Out to tea*

Tracey's and Jane's mothers had no objection to them accepting Mrs Mirza's invitation.

'One good turn deserves another,' said Tracey's mother. 'Mind you behave nicely, and offer to help wash up.'

'Oh, *Mum*!' said Tracey. 'Of course we will.'

Much the same sort of conversation was going on in Jane's house.

'It's very kind of them to ask you, so see that you are model guests, and don't be back too late.'

'Oh Mum, you do *fuss* so!' exclaimed Jane, but she hugged her mother, because – really – it was rather nice to be fussed over, though Jane didn't want to admit it.

'It seems rather a shame that Susan hasn't been

asked as well,' her mother went on. 'After all, she did just as much of the finding as you did.'

'But she wouldn't come to the Police Station,' Jane explained, 'and we couldn't very well tell them about her, or it would have seemed like asking for another invitation.'

'Why wouldn't she go with you?'

'I'm not sure,' said Jane slowly. 'I think she doesn't like policemen much.'

'She'd have liked the ones you met that day, from what you tell me. And look how kind they were about letting us know where you were, and bringing you home afterwards.'

'I know. I'll tell her all about that and see if I can get her to change her mind.'

Jane chose her moment carefully. She was bothered because Susan evidently disliked, or was even afraid of, the police. It was not a Brownie attitude at all, and one that a Sixer ought to put right if possible, she was sure.

'You know, Tracey and I had such fun the other day,' she began. 'After you'd gone home, I mean.'

'Good,' said Susan.

Jane told her about their time at the Police Station; the tea and chocolate biscuits, the messages to their families, and the final grand ride home in the police car. 'They couldn't have been kinder. It was a pity you missed it all,' she finished.

'I don't mind missing it a bit,' said Susan. 'Anyway it's all over and done with now.'

'Not really. Tracey and I are going to tea with the Mirza family at Belleview Mansions. You could have come too.'

'Belleview Mansions? Thank goodness I wasn't asked,' said Susan, obviously meaning it.

Jane was puzzled. 'But there are no police there.'

'That's all *you* know,' said Susan.

'What d'you mean?'

'Well – you know that boy Trevor?'

'The leader of the Gang?'

'Yes. Well, he lives there for a start. And several of the others. And when Bill —'

'Your brother?'

'Yes, was friends with them, they were always up to something, and the police were in and out of that place half the day and night —'

'But if the boys had been doing wrong —'

'Bill hadn't,' Susan said quickly. 'He said not. And he doesn't tell lies.'

'If only you could tell me what *did* happen,' Jane pleaded.

Susan sighed. 'All right, if you're interested. The Gang broke into a shop one night and stole a few things —'

'Broke into — !' Jane quickly hid her horror. She could see it would not be helpful.

'But Bill didn't. They made him be a look-out. Absolutely *made* him. He was much the youngest. And the others got caught, and that Trevor blamed Bill and a policeman came to our house and gave him a dreadful talking to. A warning, he called it. He was as stern as anything.'

Secretly Jane felt on the policeman's side, but she didn't say so. 'What did your Mum and Dad think?'

'They were on *his* side – the policeman's – too, and said if Bill hadn't done anything really awful, they didn't want him to start. Bill shut himself up in his room for hours. Oh, it was awful. I never want to see a policeman again. And as for that terrible Belleview Mansions, thank goodness it's you going there, not me. I only hope you enjoy it.'

Jane could see Susan didn't want to talk about policemen any more, so she only asked. 'What's so terrible about the place?'

'They're high-rise flats.'

'What's that?'

'Just what it sounds. Blocks of flats they've built up and up and up. No gardens. Nowhere to play. No pets allowed. Everybody shut up together like animals in cages.'

'Susan, you make it sound awful!'

'I tell you, it is awful. In a way I don't blame Trevor and his lot for doing stupid things. There's nothing else for them *to* do. I expect you'll enjoy yourself all right. The Mirzas sound nice. And I'd like to have seen those dear little boys again, but —' Susan shuddered.

Jane reported this conversation to Tracey.

'I still think you might have let *me* talk to her,' Tracey said. 'She is my friend, after all.'

'Mine too,' said Jane, 'and anyway it doesn't much matter who says what. She's still afraid of the police and of Trevor's Gang. She's truly glad she's not going out to tea with us.'

'Well, I'm truly glad I am,' said Tracey.

'Me too,' said Jane. She paused. 'I *think*.'

Though when the day came, the sun was so warm, and out-of-doors so inviting that it almost seemed a shame to be doing anything inside.

They had no difficulty in finding Belleview Mansions. As Tracey said, once you knew vaguely where they were it would be impossible *not* to find them. Four tall, tall narrow blocks of flats towered up into the blue sky.

They stood and stared.

'They don't look real somehow,' Jane said at last. 'More like the kind of things you make with bricks.'

'The kind that fasten together, or the whole thing would fall down long before you got to the top,' said Tracey.

Jane had been counting. 'Fourteen floors.'

'And the Mirzas' is the twelfth. How awful.'

'I don't think my legs will carry me that far,' said Jane.

Her legs didn't have to. Inside the building

was a bare stone hall. But in the hall there was a lift.

'Do you suppose we're allowed to use it?' Jane asked.

'Of course. Come on.' Tracey dragged her into the lift and closed the door. 'Look, buttons with numbers. Press twelve.'

'Press it yourself.' Jane was not over-fond of lifts.

Tracey was braver. Soon they were rattling slowly upwards. Two – three – four — seven – eight – nine —

'Ten, eleven, *twelve*, thank goodness!' said Jane stepping quickly out of the lift. They were in a bare corridor containing a number of doors. One had a card marked 'Mirza' next to the bell.

Before they could ring it the door was flung open and Farida stood there beaming. 'Come in! Come in!' They were swept inside and greeted by her mother. Mumtas and Behal paused in a game of clambering over the furniture to smile shyly. An elder brother appeared and was introduced as Khalid. Farida showed them proudly over the flat. The rooms were tidy and sparkling clean, but each time Jane looked out of a window she felt as if she were living in a strange land, disconnected from her own. The road lay such a very long way beneath them; the people and cars and buses looked like toys. It was a surprise to meet yet one more member of the family, a fat little baby girl asleep in her carry-cot.

Mr Mirza was on shiftwork so did not appear for tea. Even so, fitting everyone round the table was a squash.

It was a delicious tea. As well as bread and butter and jam and sponge-cake, there were foreign delicacies the Brownies had never tasted before. Like Farida, Khalid's English was good, and they soon found plenty to say. Mrs Mirza spoke little, but smiled a great deal and was pleased when they ate up her tea. Afterwards she was at first shocked at the idea of her visitors helping to wash up, but when they insisted she was glad to let them, because the baby woke up and began to wail for *her* tea.

'Hush! Hush!' said Farida anxiously, scooping her small sister out of the cot. 'It's Mr Paxton next door,' she explained to Tracey. 'The walls are thin, and he complains if we make too much noise.'

Tracey thought of the noise that she and her brother Johnnie and their friends often made at home, and was even more thankful she did not live in a flat.

Khalid said goodnight and went off to play with some friends.

'He's lucky,' said Farida. 'He's allowed out later than I am.'

'How long can you stay out?' Tracey asked. She had been hoping for a long time someone would suggest they went out to play.

Farida looked at her watch. 'Not long enough to make it worth while going now,' she said regretfully. 'It takes so long to get to the park, you see.'

'Isn't there somewhere nearer you could be?'

'No.'

'No playground?'

'No. There's going to be, I think, on the waste-ground behind the flats, but it hasn't been made yet.'

'Then where do you go when you want to be out for just a little while?'

'I don't,' said Farida simply. 'I stay in, mostly.'

The very thought made Tracey's long energetic legs feel twitchy.

'Anyhow there's plenty to do,' said Farida. 'With

the baby and Behal and Mumtas. We make up games we can play here.'

Jane thought of the garden at home. It was tiny, but at least there had always been room for a sandpit, and a swing. She felt sorry for the little boys who had no chance to enjoy such things. No wonder they never stopped climbing the furniture or racing about on hands and knees. They must be full of bounce they couldn't get rid of.

It had been arranged that Mr Robinson, Tracey's father, should come and fetch the girls home. It was nearly time for him to arrive.

'One last game before the boys' bedtime,' Tracey suggested, and quickly invented one in which she was a donkey keeper, Farida and Jane were the donkeys on all fours, and Mumtas and Behal raced them enthusiastically round the sitting-room.

Of course the little boys fell off and rolled on the floor and screamed with laughter.

Thump!

The loud knock on the wall made everyone jump.

Thump – thump! It came again.

'Mr Paxton,' whispered Farida. 'We must be quiet!'

A rebelling feeling rose in Tracey. It was bad enough to have to stay indoors, but to have to be quiet as well was impossible.

Something would have to be done about it.

And she would do it!

4 *Ideas – and trouble*

She was still feeling indignant when the door bell rang. Her father had come to fetch them. Goodbyes were said and the Brownies left.

'You will come again won't you?' begged Farida.

'Your turn to come to us,' said Tracey. 'And we'll go into the park she thought privately, and run and run and *run*!'

'Did you have a good time?' Mr Robinson asked on the way home.

'Yes – in a way, but —'

'They're awfully nice, but —'

'What are these "buts" about?'

Tracey and Jane did their best to explain.

'Imagine having no garden —'

'And no park —'

'And a gang of rough boys has bagged the only bit of open space near —'

'They can't even play at home —'

'Because of a cross old man next door —'

'Who thumps on the wall —'

'My legs,' declared Tracey, 'have never in all their lives felt so *do*-ish, as they did up in that flat.'

'Mine were the same,' Jane agreed, 'and they're not usually all that keen on doing. It's because they knew there was no escape.'

'Dreadful,' said Tracey with a shudder. 'Dad, why do they build places like those for living in?'

'Why indeed?' said Mr Robinson. 'There's been a great deal about it in the papers recently. A lot of people are beginning to think high-rise flats are a mistake. Especially for children.'

'So do I,' said Jane. 'That poor Farida.'

'Why is she "poor" especially?' asked Mr Robinson.

'She has to help her mother so much. She really does, with two little brothers —'

'*And* a baby.'

'She's either looking after them while her mother is shopping —'

'Or shopping while her mother stays at home.'

'The shops are quite a long way away, you see. Too far really for the little ones to walk.'

'Now if there was somewhere she could take them to play—'

'I thought the little boys gave everyone the slip and managed to get to the park all by themselves the other day,' said Mr Robinson.

'They did but only just. And they were much too tired to enjoy themselves when they got there.'

'Or to walk back.'

The problem was discussed all the way home, and Tracey thought about it long after they had dropped Jane. Something ought to be done to help families like the Mirzas. But what? And who could actually do it? She fussed during her bath and on her way to bed till her mother told her that fretting never helped anyone.

'I don't want to fret, I want to *do* something,' Tracey agreed.

Her mother had an idea. 'Why don't you tell Miss Anderson about it? She takes an interest in all sorts of social work. She might know someone – or have an idea ... Mrs Robinson's voice trailed away uncertainly. She was mostly trying to soothe Tracey.

But Tracey jumped out of bed again and hugged her mother. 'Brown Owl! Of *course*, she's the person. She always manages something. Why didn't I think of that before? Oh, *clever* old Mum!' She hugged her again.

'Not so much of the "old", thank you,' said her mother, but not really minding. 'Now do get back into bed and settle down, or you'll be too worn out to do anything about anything tomorrow.'

But by the next morning Tracey had already made her plans. She would tell Brown Owl the whole story – perhaps before the next meeting actually began – surely between them the Pack could think of something helpful to do. That was it! a Pack Venture. Just the thing for the Easter holidays. And she'd thought of it! Well, almost all of it.

She wondered whether she'd tell Jane of her plan or not. She finally decided not. In some ways it had been more fun when Jane had been her Second. Then she had always been ready to listen to Tracey and back her up. Now, in rather an annoying way, she often had ideas of her own. Sometimes she told them first to Susan – instead of to Tracey. Well, this time Jane wouldn't have the chance to interfere. Tracey would start everything off herself.

She even thought of visiting Brown Owl privately in her home to be sure she got the whole story. But the next meeting was only two days away, so it hardly seemed worth it.

But the day before the meeting Tracey could control her impatience no longer.

'I'm going to pop round and see if Jane's in,' she told her mother. 'I shan't be long.'

On the way, she imagined her friend's surprise and admiration at Tracey's plan to make the Mirzas' cause a brownie one. Jane would certainly become her old self again.

But Tracey was in for a shock. When she knocked politely at the front door, Jane's mother said, 'How nice to see you, Tracey. Do go round to the garden and join the others.'

'What others?' said Tracey quickly.

'Rosemary and Susan. They've been talking Brownies, I think.'

'Oh,' said Tracey, not very pleased. 'Perhaps I'll come again another day—'

But it was too late to escape. Cheerful voices were heard on the concrete path that led to the back garden. Jane appeared.

'Hell-*o*, Tracey! What luck, you coming today.'

'It wasn't luck,' Tracey began, 'I had something to tell you, and—'

But Jane, who seemed strangely excited, cut her short. 'Don't worry about whatever *that* was. Come on round to the back with us. *We've* got something to tell *you*.'

Reluctantly, after greeting Rosemary, her own Second, and Susan, Tracey followed them to the garden. This was not at all how she had planned things.

Jane sat on the swing where she had evidently been perched before. Rosemary and Susan sat on the see-saw. Tracey sat on the grass. There seemed to be nowhere else. It was dry, but she didn't much like the feeling that the others could look down on her.

'Now,' said Jane, 'shall we tell you our news, or will you tell us yours first?'

'Oh, mine can wait,' said Tracey, now determined to keep her secret. 'It's not important. What have you three been talking about?'

She saw them look at each other.

Jane took the lead. 'About the Mirzas, and other families like them living in those flats.'

Tracey suddenly became very alert.

'After you'd gone home, Tracey, I went on thinking who could help us until suddenly I saw we'd been idiots not to realise that this was a *Brownie* sort of thing.'

'But —' began Tracey. And then was silent, with difficulty.

'Those children – the small ones – need playing with, and taking to the park, and given some fun. Surely, if everyone helped, we could do some of that. I expect the Mums and Dads would have to join in but Brown Owl's good at getting round *them*. She's the person to talk to first. So I decided we ought to get together and have a discussion, and then we could decide how to make Brown Owl see how important it was, and how it would be a splendid Pack Venture.'

Tracey was now pink with indignation. Her own

(well, almost her own) lovely ideas, taken over by another Six. And with Rosemary helping them!

'If we took it in turns,' Rosemary now said from the see-saw, 'it wouldn't be such hard work. And we thought some of us might have push-chairs we could lend for the very little ones —'

'And we could show them all sorts of out-of-door games they don't know,' put in Susan.

Jane looked at Tracey. (Rather proudly, Tracey thought.) 'Well, what do you think of our idea?'

'Yours!' gasped Tracey. 'But they're *my* ideas!' (Most of them, anyway, she told herself.) 'I'd thought of all this. Ages ago.'

'There haven't been ages,' Jane pointed out. 'Only a few days.'

'It's seemed ages,' said Tracey. 'Look, it's simply no good you thinking that – The other day I very nearly went to Brown Owl to tell her about all this.'

'Why didn't you quite?' asked Rosemary, in a voice Tracey didn't like.

'It didn't seem worth worrying her. She's an awfully busy person, you know, and the meeting's only tomorrow.'

'Does it really matter,' said Susan, 'who thought of what, as long as it works?'

'Yes it does!' Tracey snapped, before she could stop herself.

'I don't think it does,' Jane said, swaying a little on the swing. 'Let's hear all your ideas in case you had any we haven't thought of. Then we can join them all up, and—'

'And you can pretend they were all yours,' finished Tracey furiously. 'No thank *you*.' She jumped up from the grass.

Susan had been watching and listening with some astonishment. A new Brownie, she had recently been taught that the Pack worked all together, no one thinking of themselves, but of other people. Tracey's face, red with anger, and her brimming eyes, reminded her of the miserable and unco-operative Tracey she had first known in hospital. She said nothing.

Rosemary, too, thought it wiser not to speak. She looked at Jane a little anxiously.

Jane did her best to make a joke of it all. 'Aren't we idiots, worrying about who had the idea? Susan's quite right. It doesn't matter. We'll probably think of lots of other things presently. Tracey, why don't you stay to tea? We're having jelly.'

But Tracey cared nothing for jelly. Her only thought was to leave before she cried with anger. 'I said I wouldn't be long,' she said. 'I'm off now. So you can go on talking about *my* ideas for as long as you like.'

With which words she stamped angrily off.

5 *Pack Venture*

'Have a good meeting!' said Mrs Robinson cheerfully, as Tracey set out after tea next day.

'Thanks, I will,' she answered. Privately she thought, 'I know I'm not going to. Those other three are going to be horrid about everything.'

As a matter of fact, the 'other three' were not horrid at all, even though Tracey had not behaved very well the day before; but she had made up her mind so firmly they were going to be that she found it difficult to be pleasant.

'Ah, there you are,' said Jane as soon as she saw her. 'We thought we ought to catch Brown Owl before the meeting actually begins and warn her we need time to discuss some important business. What do you think?'

'I'm not stopping you,' said Tracey.

'Jane meant all of us – you as well,' Rosemary explained.

Tracey was tempted. More than anything she wanted to join in. But she had the feeling she was being invited as an extra person, instead of being the one who should naturally explain everything. So she said, 'It doesn't need all of us to speak to Brown Owl.'

Susan said, 'Oh, come on, Trace. It'll be much more fun if you're in on it.'

She had meant to be kind and persuading, but Tracey chose to take offence. 'What do you mean "*if* I'm in on it"? Have you forgotten I was one of the people who found the boys? *And* went to the Police Station. *And* to tea at the flats. In fact, when I think of it, I don't know why you think you're part of this at all.'

Susan went red. 'I only meant – I didn't think —' She caught a warning look from Jane which plainly meant, 'Don't say any more.'

Rosemary took a breath but there was not time to say anything. Perhaps Brown Owl, who had a way

of seeing and hearing more than you'd think possible, had noticed an awkwardness going on in that corner of the room. Anyhow she held her hand up for silence earlier than usual. One by one other hands shot up, the talking trailed away, and the meeting began. Presently, she asked, 'Is there anything anyone thinks we ought to discuss?' She looked round the circle, paying especial attention to Rosemary, Jane, Susan and Tracey.

No one was sure who should speak out first, so Tracey, seeing her chance, took it. 'Yes, there is,' she said firmly. 'Something's happened and I think we ought to do something about it, and funnily enough some other people had the same idea.'

If Brown Owl saw some odd looks being exchanged, she took no notice of them, but only said, 'Let's hear all about it then. You begin, Tracey.'

So Tracey, feeling better now that she was at the centre of things, started to give everyone an account of how the little Mirza boys had been found in the park. Presently Susan broke in with a detail that had been forgotten, and in spite of a scowl from Tracey, Jane too, began to fill in parts of the story. Questions were asked, especially about the Police Station, in which all the Brownies were most interested, and there were sighs of relief when the happy ending was reached.

'Yes, but that's only part of it,' Tracey said. Then she and Jane described their visit to the Belleview Mansions, and tried hard to make everyone understand how unlucky the families were who lived in those conditions. A great deal of sympathetic talking broke out, and it was clear that people agreed that the Pack ought to help if possible.

'Couldn't we make it a Pack Venture?' Rosemary pleaded.

'I don't see why we shouldn't do *something* to help,' Brown Owl said slowly. 'But you know, we can't put everything right overnight and by ourselves. And we don't have to. Now I'll tell you something that *you* don't know, and which will make you feel better. A lot of people are worried by the lack of playing space for children in high-rise flats, and I know some of them in this area. Plans have been made for improvements. First, the rough ground behind the flats is going to be made into a proper adventure playground with a supervisor. That will help enormously.'

'But it will take ages, won't it?' asked Tracey. 'When will it be ready?'

'In time for the summer holidays, it's hoped. I know that seems a long way away now, but at least the playground will be there when it's most wanted. The other thing that's being done – and this project has already been started – is that one of the basements of the flats is being converted into a huge playroom for the little ones under school age. There'll be room for them to do big paintings, and get messy with clay and Plasticine, and enjoy a sand-tray, and play rowdy games – all the things they can't do in their flats.'

'Will they be by themselves?' asked Tracey thinking of the noise and mess and muddle there would be.

'No, no. The mothers in that block have formed a sort of club. They're going to take it in turns to look after the children at certain hours, so that there's always somebody in charge.'

'That's a good idea,' said Susan. 'Because when it's *not* their turn, they can go to the shops without having to take the children every time.'

'Exactly. I'm sure it will work out splendidly once it gets going. The only snag is, the basement won't be ready till next term. So they are still going to have a difficult time during these holidays—'

'*Unless*—' broke in several eager voices.

Brown Owl smiled. 'I know what you're going to say, "unless *we* come to the rescue in some way". Well, I don't see why something shouldn't be managed. But it will mean everybody helping. And when I say "everybody", I mean your families as well. Looking after a number of small children is a most responsible business, and there must be at least one adult person in charge of an outing.'

The Brownies, though regretful, could see the point of this.

'A lot will depend,' Brown Owl pointed out, 'on how many of your parents feel they can give time to back you up in the scheme.'

There were some doubtful faces now. More than one mother had been heard to say she found the school holidays hard work, when only looking after her own family, let alone anyone else's. Most fathers, of course, worked all day and their evenings were precious. Those with gardens especially found this a busy time of year. The room became a little more quiet.

'Yes,' Brown Owl said, 'when you think seriously about it, you see it's quite a big task you want to take on. But don't let's despair. We're not thinking of providing a daily service. We have four Sixes. So if each Six could provide one play-period every week, that would make four outings for the children. And it's only for three weeks – less.'

Put like that, the plan sounded much more hopeful. Excited voices rose again. Brown Owl had to remind them that there was a whole group of people who had to be consulted before anything began: the parents of the children in the flats.

'But they'd be awfully pleased,' Tracey assured her. 'I know because of things Mrs Mirza said.'

'Just the same they must all be asked,' Brown Owl said firmly. 'You can't go scooping off people's children without permission, even to give them a good time.'

In the end it was arranged that Brown Owl would approach the families in Belleview Mansions. Every

Brownie would talk to her own parents, and they'd hold a special meeting, with as many parents attending as possible, in a few days, to see what could be worked out.

Then it was time to get down to some work, followed by a game in order to stretch the legs. All too soon the meeting had to break up.

During the next few days, everyone was very busy indeed, particularly Brown Owl who had more to do than anyone. Quite a number of mothers managed to be at the extra meeting. Some had sent notes instead of themselves, but most of the notes said they would be glad to help. Only a few said regretfully they really couldn't spare the time.

Brown Owl reported that the parents in the flats had been delighted by the offer. ('Told you so,' muttered Tracey.) A list of days and times was drawn up. The project would start next week. The first Six to start would be Tracey's own: the Pixies, supported by Mrs Robinson and another mother.

'I only hope everything goes well,' Rosemary whispered. 'It would be awful if we made a mess of the very first time.'

'Why should we?' said Tracey, but inside she, too, felt a little anxious. Suppose the children wouldn't do as they were told, or fell down and hurt themselves, or wouldn't join in the games? Oh well, the mothers would be there. For the first time, she was really glad of that.

The only thing that might spoil the fun would be the weather. It had been agreed that if it was bad the children could not go out, but games would be played instead in the bare basement. So far though it looked as if the spell of mild spring sunshine was going to last.

On *the* morning, Tracey woke up with a funny feeling in her tummy. For a moment she couldn't think why. Then she remembered: the Pixies were going to start the Venture. She looked anxiously out of the window, but there was a reassuring haze which promised warm sun later. She hurried her own breakfast, and nagged her younger brother Johnnie to get on with his, till he rebelled.

'Oh you and your Brownie nonsense!' he exclaimed in disgust. 'If I want another piece of toast I shall have it.'

'But you don't,' said Tracey quickly. 'You've had two already.'

'I feel like three today,' said Johnnie, especially, thought the agitated Tracey, to be annoying.

'We've plenty of time,' her mother said, 'especially if you help me with the washing up.'

Tracey was not pleased with this idea, but she could see it was a fair one.

At last everything was tidied away, and she and her mother set off to meet the rest of their party.

'This,' she told herself, 'is our biggest and best Pack Venture yet. An *Ad*venture.'

Little did she know just what an adventure it was to turn out to be.

6 *In the park*

At Belleview Mansions an excited group of small children waited, with their mothers. Farida was amongst them, clutching Behal with one hand and Mumtas with the other. She grinned broadly when she saw Tracey.

'What a super idea! I bet it was yours. We're going to have a great time.'

Tracey glanced uneasily at Rosemary. 'We?'

'Of course I'm coming too, I wouldn't miss it for anything,' said Farida.

'The thing is,' said Tracey, embarrassed, 'we were really only supposed to be taking the younger ones.'

'But I shall be a helper, just like you,' said Farida easily.

It really was rather awkward. 'Eight years old and

under', was the age of the children they had planned to entertain. Farida was nine.

Luckily Brown Owl herself appeared at that moment. Hastily, Tracey explained the problem.

Brown Owl looked round the group of excited faces. 'I don't think Farida is the only one who isn't strictly the right age,' she murmured.

Raising her voice, she spoke to the mothers from the flats. 'We did agree, didn't we, that eight was the age-limit?'

There was a short silence. Then one of them said, 'My Perce was nine only last week so he'd be all right wouldn't he?'

Someone else said, 'I don't think our Norah will come without her big sister.'

It was clear that a number of the children were more than eight.

'But it does seem a shame,' said Jane. 'They want to come just as much. And they're just as much shut up.'

Brown Owl looked worried. She had a quick quiet word with the Brownie mothers. It was finally decided that on this occasion Brown Owl herself would accompany the party, and see how it went with the extra numbers.

'But it's only an experiment,' she warned everybody. 'If we find we're too many, we shall have to go back to the old rule.'

Everybody nodded and smiled. The older children each held the hand of a younger. There were four push-chairs to be managed. They made quite a procession.

They were very very careful about crossing roads.

As soon as they were in the park, the children were allowed to run free. And run was the word! Most of them tore round in wild circles, just shouting.

One or two stood about looking lost.

'Off you go,' said Mrs Robinson. 'As long as you don't leave the park you can run where you like.'

The children looked uncertain. At last one whispered, 'Please Miss, are we really allowed on the grass?'

'Yes, as long as you don't swing on the trees or pick any flowers.'

Hesitating at first the children moved away. Then they found the springy grass under their feet. Soon they were running and shouting with the rest.

Only one small girl stayed close to the grown-up party, her thumb in her mouth.

'What's your name, dear?' Brown Owl asked.

The thumb came out for just long enough for the little girl to whisper 'Norah,' and then went in again.

'Our Norah,' said Brown Owl. 'That means there'll be a big sister somewhere. Rosemary, see if you can find her.'

Rosemary ran off and soon returned with Norah's sister Mary.

'She's always like that. She likes watching best.'

'Then she shall watch,' said Brown Owl.

For some time everyone dashed about without much purpose. Then Tracey thought it was time to organise something. The Brownies collected the children together and suggested a game of 'tag'. Some of the younger ones were not sure how to play. Some others had done enough running about for the time being. So the more energetic ones joined in the game. The rest straggled back to the grown-ups. One Brownie mother showed several how to turn

somersaults on the soft grass. Mrs Robinson, explaining carefully that daisies were different from the flowers in the beds, made a daisy chain. Soon several children were picking daisies to make their own. Brown Owl had brought two skipping-ropes and was soon showing eager borrowers how to use them.

When the 'tag' players were exhausted they joined the rest. Everyone sat down. Mrs Robinson produced some bags of crisps. Everyone munched a few of these while she told them a short but exciting story. Then Brown Owl divided them into teams and they ran several races. Behal fell down and grazed his knee. Brown Owl was ready with antiseptic cream and plaster. Farida was very useful when it came to telling Behal when it was time to stop crying. In fact everyone agreed that having the older children there was a good idea, and that the age-limit should be raised to ten.

A general groan of disappointment greeted the news that it was time to start for home. There was a hunt for cardigans and jackets, a quick look round to make sure they'd left no litter, such as crisp-packets behind, a careful counting of heads, and off they went.

'Well, how did it go?' Jane asked Tracey that afternoon, having come round to her house especially to enquire.

'Fine,' she answered. 'Why, did you think something would go wrong?'

Jane wondered if she could ever say the right thing to Tracey these days. She hid a sigh of exasperation. 'Of course not. I just wondered if you could pass on any tips to us?'

Tracey spoke slowly. She couldn't resist it. 'I don't think so. Of course I expect you know there are many more of them than we expected? Brown Owl has decided to let the up-to-tens join in.'

'Why? Was she there too?' Jane asked in surprise.

'Just for the first day. She won't be always, she says. Oh, and Mum took some crisps for elevenses.'

'That's a good idea, I hadn't thought of that. Thanks. Did you take anything else?'

'Brown Owl took skipping-ropes. They liked those.'

'Goodness. I haven't even got one. I don't know if

anyone else has. Could we – would you lend us yours?'

'I suppose I could,' said Tracey ungraciously. She didn't see why she should supply apparatus for Jane's Six. She went off unwillingly to fetch it.

'I want it taken care of, mind,' she said when she returned with it.

'Of course. We've got two balls between us. They should help.' Jane looked worried, all the same.

'I shouldn't fuss if I were you,' Tracey said. 'There's nothing to it.' She wasn't going to admit that she herself had fussed dreadfully till it was all safely over.

But for poor Jane, things did not go so well. For one thing their second was away from home, so she had to manage without. For another there was no Brown Owl that day and it happened that she had not met either of the two mothers in the party.

However, all was well to begin with. After the first dashing was over, the Brownies showed the other older ones how to play 'Cat and Mouse' and 'I sent a letter to my love', while the mothers played younger games with the smaller children. Then there was a general rest during which they ate chocolate beans and played 'I spy'.

It was then the troubles began. Tracey's skipping-rope was produced and a fierce squabble broke out over who was to use it. The mothers settled this but not before some punching and pushing had taken place.

Then Jane and Susan tried to start a ball game. Just as it was getting exciting, Susan dropped an easy catch.

'Idiot,' said Jane, laughing.

But Susan wasn't laughing. She was staring towards the bushes, her face quite pale.

Jane bent to pick the ball off the ground. 'Come on, wake up!' she hissed. 'What's the matter?'

'The Gang!' gasped Susan. 'I can see them. Lurking!'

Jane did not at all like the word 'lurking', but she said bravely, 'Nonsense. They just happen to be here.' And picked up the ball.

'Not them,' Susan insisted. 'I know that —'

'Later,' said Jane briefly, and threw the ball. But though the game continued peacefully for several minutes, now she too, was uncomfortably aware of peering faces close by.

Then somebody hurled the ball rather wildly. No one could catch it. It bounced into the bushes.

Instantly a figure leapt out, grabbed the ball, and disappeared again.

'Here!' cried Jane. 'That's ours.'

'Careful!' Susan begged. 'It's that Trevor!'

'I don't care. It's our ball —' Jane ran towards the bushes.

But now the Gang was running too. Towards the park gates.

Trevor jeered over his shoulder. 'Finding's keeping!'

'Get the grown-ups!' Jane ordered. But they were too late. By the time the two mothers had hurried to the scene the incident was over. There was no sign of the Gang.

Or the Brownies' ball.

Everybody was indignant, but a number of the children from the flats knew Trevor and his ways only too well.

'Better not get across *him*, Miss,' one of them

advised a Brownie mother. 'That Gang can get really tough!'

Of course they had the other ball, and anyhow there were plenty of other games to be played. But somehow the morning had been spoiled.

'They're all much bigger than we are,' Jane said at the end of it. 'You'd think they'd leave us alone.'

'Not them, they're bullies,' said Susan. 'And they don't like it that we have all this fun, and no one's doing anything for them. That's what they say.'

'Oh dear,' sighed Jane. 'It is difficult to please everyone.'

'We'd better tell Brown Owl what happened, in case they interfere another time.'

'Yes,' agreed Jane comforted. 'And she'll know what to do. Somehow she always does.'

7 *Party plans*

Brown Owl had a quiet word with the mothers concerned, and Trevor's Gang did not spoil another outing. Certainly they appeared from time to time, sometimes only to shout out insulting remarks, occasionally to ride headlong through the middle of games on bicycles or roller skates. But although they made a great deal of noise, they did no real harm. The Brownies, knowing the grown-ups in their parties were on the watch, stopped worrying.

The good weather went on and on which was a great help towards making the Venture a success. Several children from the flats were planning to become Brownies. Farida was particularly keen.

'If only they'll let me. Something to look forward to every week!'

'She hasn't much else,' Rosemary said privately to Tracey.

'I know. And sometimes I feel her mother expects her to do far too much. Then I think, "How could Mrs Mirza manage without Farida?"'

As the mornings went on, different activities were introduced. The Gnomes had a father who owned a grocery and confectionery shop. He produced some clean sacks. That day sack-races were a feature of the fun.

The following week the Imps took flower-pots to the park, and everybody practised 'flower-pot-walking'. Skipping had already become a great craze; and even the smallest members were becoming more clever with a ball.

'You know,' Tracey said, 'lots of them could soon take their Athlete's badges – if only they were Brownies.'

Jane's mind had been following a different track. It was the second turn of the Elves to organise the outing. During the break, conversation had turned to Christmas parties.

'They have great parties in the hospital,' Susan

said. 'Some of the others told me. They decorate the wards, and have a Christmas tree, and play the kind of games that people can manage even when they're in bed.'

'I've never been to a Christmas party,' said a little girl from the flats, 'or a party at all. What *is* a party?'

Somebody old enough to be at school described the one they had there at the end of term. 'A huge tea, and lots of games. You know, musical bumps and oranges and lemons – things like that.'

Jane saw Farida's face. She wore a happy remembering expression. Of course musical bumps or oranges and lemons would be quite impossible in a small flat with somebody next door ready to bang on the wall if there were a noise. Farida could only have a party if there were someone else to organise it. And those too young to go to school, didn't even know what a party *was*!

The beginnings of an idea came to her. She kept it to herself till she was walking home with Susan.

'I say, what about a party?'

'A party?' Susan looked blank.

'For our last outing? An extra one. With everybody there.'

'But Christmas is over,' Susan objected.

'You can have a party any time,' said Jane. They were passing Tracey's house. 'Let's ask Tracey what she thinks.'

Susan hesitated. 'She thinks she ought to have thought of everything first.'

'She hasn't this time,' said Jane firmly. 'I have. But she's good at thinking of all the extras. Come on!' She strode up the short path to Tracey's door. Susan was a good friend, but not so enthusiastic about things as Tracey, Jane had found.

Tracey was in. She seemed quite pleased to see them. 'How did this morning go?'

'Oh fine,' said Jane. 'No trouble. But I've had an idea.'

'Another?' said Tracey, raising her eyebrows.

Jane wondered whether it was worth being annoyed by Tracey's tone or not. She decided not. 'Well, only half an idea,' she said generously. 'I expect you'll have all the other halves.'

'You can't have more than two halves on one

whole,' Susan began in a practical way, but the others had no time to listen to her, for Tracey had at once approved the idea of a party.

'An *Easter* party,' she said excitedly. 'An out-of-door one in the park.'

'With an enormous picnic —'

'Everybody bringing something —'

'And sports. Games. Races.'

'You'll have to mind the Gang,' Susan warned.

'There'll be all the mothers there,' said Tracey, 'or as many as we can get. And Brown Owl, because we can have it instead of a regular meeting —'

'And it will be a wonderful finish-up to our Venture!' Jane could see it all.

'Suppose it rains?' asked Susan.

'Oh, don't think of so many objections,' said Tracey impatiently. 'Could it be dressing-up d'you think?'

Jane considered. 'Expensive. And not much time.'

'True,' Tracey admitted with regret. Then she cheered up. 'What about masks?'

'Fine! Paper masks. Everyone to make their own.'

'And one of the mothers to be judge.'

'If there's a competition, there has to be a prize,' Susan pointed out.

'Or points for the Sixes,' said Tracey. 'The one with the most at the end to have one prize.'

'But the children from the flats don't belong to Sixes,' Susan pointed out.

This was true. That idea was abandoned. 'Anyway prizes aren't all that important,' said Jane. 'We can work it all out somehow.'

'It'll have to be with Brown Owl,' Tracey said.

'Of course. Let's go and see her.'

'Now, this minute?'

'Why not?'

'Because now this minute is dinner time,' said Mrs Robinson appearing unexpectedly. 'I'm sure Jane and Susan ought to be at home. And poor Brown Owl has to eat as well, you know. Why don't you ring her up from the telephone box later, and see if there is a convenient time for you to call?'

As Mrs Robinson was putting carrots on the table for her family as she spoke, and Jane and Susan indeed knew they were late, her suggestion was adopted. Brown Owl said they could look in about tea-time for a short visit before she would have to go out.

Although of course they were not in uniform, it was three tidy Brownies who arrived on Brown Owl's doorstep sharp at four o'clock.

'Better start tea before we talk,' she said briskly. 'Who's going to brew it? And I'll need someone to lay the table, and somebody else to carry things through from the kitchen.'

There was a bustling about to get ready. Susan found herself carrying banana sandwiches, egg sandwiches, a sponge-cake with jam in the middle and a plate of chocolate biscuits. There seemed a great deal of food for only four people, but Brown Owl knew about Brownies' appetites.

'Now then,' she said, as soon as they were seated round the table. 'You talk while I pour.'

Soon she heard all about the party.

'We can do it, can't we?' pleaded Tracey. 'With *everybody* helping, there'd be nothing to it.'

'I wouldn't say that,' Brown Owl disagreed. She knew better than anyone how much organising Ventures take, even when everyone is helping.

All the same, she didn't say 'No', which was a hopeful sign. But she did suggest that mothers and some fathers had been asked to help a good deal already. She thought, for instance, the Brownies themselves should prepare the food.

'No reason why you shouldn't, and the practice would be very helpful for anyone wanting to take her Cook or Hostess badge.'

'Why?' Susan wanted to know.

'A "cook" must be able to make scones or small cakes, among other things. Part of the Hostess badge is to welcome and look after a guest or guests in your own home or at a party, or at a Brownie "event". But you must prepare the refreshments yourself.'

'Better and better,' said Jane. 'We can *all* take our Hostess badges.'

'You also have to write some letters,' Brown Owl reminded her.

Tracey groaned. 'Always there's writing to be done!'

Brown Owl only laughed at her. 'Just because you're an outdoor person it doesn't mean you can't use your hands!'

At that moment Tracey had just used her hand to fill her mouth with sponge-cake, so she was unable to argue. Also, she wasn't sure she could think of anything useful to say.

The Pack greeted the idea of an Easter Party as a grand finish to their Venture with great enthusiasm. A date was fixed. Brown Owl said she would book the hall where they had their meetings just in *case* it rained. Several mothers who had helped with the Venture said they'd like to help at the party too. A number of Brownies who had not thought of taking Cook or Hostess badges before, determined now to do so. The children from the flats were delighted, their parents even more so.

News of the proposed event soon spread. Most people thought it a very good plan.

But not everyone.

Trevor met Farida on the stairs in Belleview Mansions. He gave her the kind of smile that was not pleasant.

'We know all about your silly party,' he told her. 'If you try to have it, we're coming too. To wreck it!'

8 *The party starts*

Consternation! Again the Brownies flew to Brown Owl, again she was soothing. 'There'll be lots of us there, remember. No need to worry.'

It was difficult not to, but the thing that helped most, was being busy. For there were lots of things to plan for the party. First there would be a grand procession of the paper masks. Then games and competitions. Owing to practice everyone was quite good at sack-races, and walking on flower-pots. There would be skipping competitions too, all manner of team games, and, an unexpected item, a treasure hunt for Easter eggs. The kind father who sold sweets said he would provide lots of tiny eggs in bright glittery paper. These would be hidden round the park at the last minute and the team that found the most would win that game. All of this was decided at a meeting of the Sixers and their seconds with Brown Owl. They also arranged that the grown-ups concerned should sort out the teams to make it fair, allotting to each Six a selection of children from the flats, some big, some little.

Of course a very important item to be discussed was the tea. Who would bring what? It was discussed at the last full meeting before the party.

Some people had favourite things they knew they could manage: rock buns, or cornflakes – stuck together with melted chocolate. There was a large number of volunteers to produce sandwiches.

'Lovely' said Brown Owl. 'Everyone likes those, but don't let's forget those Cook's badges. Scones, for instance. What about some scone volunteers?'

One or two hands crept up doubtfully. 'Come on,' said Brown Owl. 'How about you, Tracey?'

Tracey squirmed. 'Cooking's not really my kind of *thing*,' she explained.

'All the more reason to have a try,' said Brown Owl cheerfully. 'I'll put you down for a dozen, shall I?'

Tracey gave a small groan.

Susan said her mother had just shown her how to make a treacle tart. She thought she'd be able to manage one.

Rosemary said *her* mother had recently shown her how to make a chocolate sponge-cake. 'But something went horribly wrong with mine,' she admitted ruefully. 'It turned out more like a chocolate pancake!'

It was agreed that a chocolate pancake – should the next effort prove disastrous as well – might not be so welcome as other things. Rosemary settled for tomato sandwiches.

Jane said her mother had a lot of cardboard cups. What about jellies in them?

'Yes – yes!' cried a number of voices.

Jam tarts, sugar-coated biscuits, flapjacks and crisps were added to the lists.

The subject of drinks came up. And plates and spoons to eat the jellies with.

Brown Owl, who had been looking into the matter of how much money the Pack had to spend, thought they could manage orange and lemon squash and

Coke and disposable plates, spoons and cups. She would see to all that.

'We'll take the food to the park if the weather's at all possible. If it isn't, I've booked this hall instead.'

Nobody wanted to use the hall, but it was clear that a picnic in the rain would not be much fun.

'We'll have to keep our fingers crossed for a good forecast,' said Brown Owl.

Whether it was to do with the crossed fingers or not, the sun shone . . . and shone.

On the morning of the party, the radio was turned on in many Brownie homes, in order to hear the weather forecast. 'After a bright start to the day,' said the official not-caring voice of the announcer, 'a shallow depression will move across the country from the west, bringing with it showers, some of which may be heavy.'

'Oh *no*!' wailed many voices in hearing this news.

'We might not get any showers at all,' said Mrs Robinson.

'But we might get a heavy one,' said Tracey, determined to be gloomy. Part of the gloom was due to the thought of the scone-making, which was her task for the morning.

'Let's look on the bright side,' said Mrs Robinson. 'We're going to have the party anyway, aren't we?'

'You can't have proper running-about games in the hall,' Tracey said. 'Not enough room.'

'Suppose you stopped worrying about it and made a start on those scones?'

Tracey sighed heavily. 'They're sure to be awful.'

'Nonsense! Scones are easy to make. You've seen me do them dozens of times.'

'I've seen you, but not really *looked*,' Tracey explained, unwillingly beginning to gather the ingredients. After reading the recipe from the cook book several times, and asking her mother many questions, Tracey achieved a dough.

'It doesn't seem to know how to stick together properly,' she said, at last, peering discontentedly into the bowl.

'Try a drop more milk,' her mother advised. 'Tracey – "a *drop*" I said!' she cried a minute later, as Tracey tipped the milk jug generously over the mixture.

'It'll only make them nice and soft, won't it?' she asked hopefully.

'Well —' her mother looked doubtful.

A minute later Tracey was in trouble again: 'It's all so sticky! It won't roll out!'

'I was afraid of that. Let's scatter a little flour around. It's not the best way to do things, but it might save the situation.'

It didn't. When Tracey's scones were ready to take out of the oven she got a shock. Instead of rising, each had sprawled wetly into the one next door, so that the baking tray was one soggy mess.

'Oh!' cried Tracey torn between disappointment and fury. 'Horrible *things*! I *said* I wouldn't be able to do them!'

At this unfortunate moment Johnnie bounced into the kitchen. 'What on earth —?'

'That's enough,' said his mother quickly. 'We don't need any help in here.' She tried to shoo him out of the kitchen.

'But what *is* it?'

'They were supposed to be scones, but they went wrong,' admitted Tracey sulkily.

Johnnie hooted with laughter. 'Scones! I thought it was that stuff Dad sticks on wallpaper with!'

Mrs Robinson hustled him off, but not before Tracey was nearly in tears of humiliation.

'Never mind, darling, we'll throw this lot away, and I'll whip up some more in a moment in case they're counting on them. You can make some sandwiches – egg ones – they always go well. Then you'll feel you've done something yourself.'

Things were not entirely successful in other families either. Some flapjacks got burned, some rock buns turned out much more like rocks than buns, a pile of tomato sandwiches got sprinkled with sugar instead of salt by mistake. But one or two things go wrong at all the best parties, and by lunch-time baskets were loaded with provisions, and Brownies were busily pressing uniforms, polishing shoes, putting the last touches to masks.

Rosemary stuck her head out of the window. 'The sun's not so bright as it was. And it's cooler.'

'But it's still fine,' said her mother. 'Don't forget to take your mac.' It had previously been decided everyone could do this – they would be sat on if the weather was good, worn if it wasn't.

Soon a number of smart though laden Brownies met at the park. Only the Sixers had gone with Brown Owl to the flats to fetch the visitors.

When the Brownie pack got there they had a surprise, for the guests were also loaded with food.

'But we didn't mean you to contribute anything!' said Brown Owl.

'But it's only right that we should,' said a mother seeing her children off. 'A lovely time you've given them, so we thought we'd all help.'

'What shall we *do*?' Jane whispered to Brown Owl on the way to the park. 'We've got enough food to feed an army!'

'Better too much than too little,' said Brown Owl. 'And remember that running round will give everyone a tremendous appetite.'

All the same, when all the food was put together, the mothers in charge of it were rather flabbergasted. 'Lovely things – look, shortbread, and an iced Easter-cake, ham-rolls – but so *much*!'

Brown Owl saw Tracey taking the things out of her own basket. Amongst them was the beautiful batch of scones, tall, light, pale brown and shiny on top.

'There, Tracey, I knew you'd manage!' said Brown Owl admiringly.

'Actually I —' Tracey began. Then a dreadful temptation came to her. She glanced round quickly to see where her mother was. Safely far away. 'They weren't all that difficult,' she muttered. Then she had to turn her face away quickly so that Brown Owl shouldn't see her go red with shame.

She was glad to put on her mask and join in the parade.

It certainly was an extraordinary sight – a number of small people marching solemnly in a circle wearing all manner of disguises. Many people remembering it was an Easter party had come as chickens. There were also rabbits – easy to identify by the long ears, and a number of other animals, not too easy to be sure about. Some of the boys had fierce villainous-looking masks, some of the girls had pretty ones decorated with flowers. As there was a rule that no one must pay more than five pence towards the materials, a great deal of making-do had gone on. All the same it was very difficult for the mother who was judging to

make up her mind. When she did it was to declare the winner a very shy little girl from the flats who had come as an elephant, complete with a trunk made of hosepipe. Everyone was pleased by the choice and there was an outbreak of clapping, made all the louder by members of the public who had paused to watch the competition with first amazement, then amusement.

'And now,' announced Brown Owl, 'games. Will you get into your teams, please?'

There was a great shuffling about and many excited voices.

The Easter Party was really under way.

9 *Danger?*

The Brownies were careful not to let their party become a nuisance to anyone else who might want to stroll in the park. All the same, quite a lot of people stopped to watch the energetic games, and applaud the winners. Presently, though, most of them moved on. The reason for this was because some white puffy clouds had for the moment hidden the sun. It was warm enough for running, but not for standing.

One of the mothers helping to spread out the enormous tea, glanced anxiously upwards. 'Do you think it's worth going on with this?'

Another, more hopeful mother, working with her,

answered, 'Oh yes, surely. I think the clouds are going the other way.'

Their work proceeded.

Meanwhile tremendous sack-races and flower-pot races and team games were taking place. There were competitions for even the youngest members of the party, so nobody felt left out.

'This must be the best party ever!' Tracey had time to whisper to Rosemary.

'As long as the rain keeps off,' she said.

Tracey, who had been too busy to do so before, looked at the sky. There was no sun to be seen, and over the trees she could see clumps of clouds arranging themselves into a long line. 'Oh it *mustn't*!' she said, and then it was time to help hide the eggs for the treasure hunt, so she raced off, forgetting the weather.

The treasure hunt was a great success. In spite of the feast they could see being prepared, everybody felt the little chocolate eggs should be eaten at once, so they were, the silver paper being carefully collected.

It was while the egg-and-spoon race (hard boiled

eggs being used) was starting that Jane plucked nervously at Brown Owl's arm. 'Don't say anything to Susan, but I've seen that Trevor, and I think the rest of the Gang is with him.'

'Thank you, Jane,' said Brown Owl, as if the news were not in the least important. 'Never mind. Just see that those little ones understand they've got to drop their eggs into the flower-pots will you?'

But after that, although she always seemed to be doing about ten other things at once, Brown Owl somehow found time to keep her eye on the crowd of older children, some on roller skates, some with bicycles, that was collecting behind the bushes. She had a quick quiet word with some of the mothers, then another with those in charge of the food. In between she blew her whistle to start the races, announced the winners, answered questions, and was in fact, her usual self.

It was just as a general game of 'twos and threes' was being arranged, that it happened.

Suddenly there was a tremendous outburst of shouts and whistles and bicycle bells. From behind the bushes exploded the Gang, quite evidently out to make trouble. With loud yells they skated or rode right through the circle of players about to start their game. Then Trevor gave an order, the Gang wheeled round and crashed back across the same ground.

The Brownies, all rather scared, and some really frightened, scattered fast. The mothers with the tea gathered protectively round it. Others went quickly to where Brown Owl was standing.

She blew her whistle very loud and long.

There is something about an authoritative blast on a whistle which tends to make everyone stop in his tracks. Even Trevor and his Gang were startled enough to come to an abrupt halt.

There was a moment's silence, Brown Owl spoke in a loud clear voice.

'Good afternoon,' she said. 'Which of you is Trevor?'

Trevor himself, as Susan noticed, tried to wriggle behind his followers. They were not standing for this.

'He is, Miss,' said several, pointing at him. He got pushed to the front in spite of himself.

'I'm glad to meet you, Trevor,' said Brown Owl,

as if she really were. 'And your friends. But we were just starting a game here – I expect you hadn't noticed.'

'They had. They did it on purpose,' hissed Susan.

'Sh!' ordered Jane sharply.

'But what *I've* noticed,' went on Brown Owl, 'is that you've all got roller skates or bicycles. I expect you're pretty good on them?'

There were shufflings of feet and ''ums' and 'ahs'. The Brownies noticed that when faced by Brown Owl, the dreaded Gang seemed suddenly smaller and much less fierce.

As there were no direct answers, she went on. 'We should very much like to see what you can do. Trevor, do you think you could arrange a short display for us?'

Trevor, uncertain, looked round at his Gang. Seeing that several members seemed quite pleased with this idea he muttered, 'I suppose so, yes.'

'We'll look forward to that very much,' said Brown Owl. 'In perhaps a quarter of an hour? Of course you'll want to do some planning of your exhibition first. You'd better do this practising on the other

TREV

side of the park so that we can't see it. Then you could let us know when you're ready, and we'll be an audience. Thank you so much.'

She spoke so firmly, as if the whole thing had already been decided that the Gang found itself making off. As they went their voices could be heard arguing about who was to perform each trick.

'Now then, where were we?' said Brown Owl cheerfully. 'Do you think you can make your circle again, just as it was? Then we can start to play.'

Susan breathed out a huge breath of relief. Somehow the Gang had failed to wreck the party. The battle was over without ever beginning. She was not sure how Brown Owl had managed this, but if she could do it once, she could do it again. She took her place ready for the game much relieved.

The clouds piled silently one upon another, moving stealthily towards the sun. They were darker now, like very *dirty* cotton wool.

Presently Trevor appeared. Brown Owl spoke to him. She blew her whistle again.

'And now,' she announced to everybody. 'We are going to have a grand display of roller-skating and trick-riding of bicycles. Sit down everybody.'

Everybody sat, and most people put on cardigans, because it was distinctly more chilly than it had been.

The display began.

It was not, honestly, a very good one. The children in the Gang had not had very much time to prepare, and a number of things went wrong, including a boy falling off his bicycle and grazing his elbow so badly that first aid had to be applied.

But the Brownies, realising the display was especially for them, clapped politely at the end of every turn.

It was under cover of a burst of clapping that Tracey whispered to Brown Owl, 'How are you going to make them go?'

'Must they go?' she murmured. 'We've more than enough food —'

'But they might go back to being awful!' said Tracey, alarmed.

'I don't think so. Not if we put it to them the right way,' Brown Owl answered. Then the clapping came to an end and they had to stop talking.

'For our last act —' Trevor announced, and a boy rode a cycle in small circles using no hands.

Brown Owl, by means of her eyebrows was making signals to the other mothers. Most of them nodded, some looked doubtful. Tracey understanding the signals felt most doubtful of all.

But when the performance was over, Brown Owl stood up and thanked Trevor and his friends formally on behalf of everybody present, for the magnificent display. Then she said, 'We are now going to have a picnic party. If you would like to join us, we would be very happy to welcome you.'

A surprised buzz broke out among the Brownies. During it Brown Owl spoke to the Gang. 'As you can see, we have a number of very young children here from Belleview Mansions. They do need a good deal of looking after. I know most of you live in the same block of flats, and know them. It would be most helpful if you could join us as organisers.'

Trevor looked surprised. 'You mean we'd be – like the grown-ups?'

'Just like the grown-ups,' agreed Brown Owl. 'Helping to see that everything goes smoothly.'

'Oh well. I see what you mean. That's different,' said Trevor in an embarrassed way. 'Isn't it?' He turned to his Gang.

There were muttered agreements. They were standing near the delicious tea. It would be hard to refuse it in any case, but as grown-up helpers —

'Of course we wouldn't want to be just like the other little kids at a kid's party,' Trevor explained, anxious to make their position clear.

'Of course not,' agreed Brown Owl. 'No question of it. Splendid. Now I expect you'd like to prop up your bicycles and take off your roller skates so that we can get started.'

When Brown Owl made suggestions in that sort of voice, they had a habit of being followed. Meekly, the Gang did as it had been asked.

The mothers were arranging everybody round the loaded plates. The Brownies, the mothers, the flat-children and the Gang were all mixed up together like one big party. Even with so many people present, there seemed to be a great deal of food.

Paper serviettes were passed round.

So were paper cups to drink from.

Everyone was ready to start eating the lovely tea.

And then, just as Brown Owl was saying 'We'll begin with sandwiches, shall we?' the first big drops of rain fell.

10 *New ideas*

'Oh!' wailed a great many voices. But Brown Owl felt there was no time for 'oh's!'.

'Please mothers, could you all help to re-pack the tea? Macs on, everyone. Brownies get into your Sixes quickly – Belleview children come over here with me. Trevor, is your party ready to move?'

In no time the tea was back in its baskets, paper tablecloths folded, everybody in macintoshes having snatched up belongings, including, of course roller skates and bicycles.

'Right, off we go!' said Brown Owl, and before the rain had had time to get properly started, the whole procession was on its way briskly out of the park. The mothers led the way, the Brownies walking in Sixes, then came Brown Owl with the children from the flats walking tidily two by two. Last of all came Trevor and his Gang, quite surprised to find themselves being so firmly organised.

The hall was not far away. In a few minutes it was full of breathless people. At first it looked as if no sort of order could be made of all the bodies struggling out of macs, the clattering of dropped roller skates, while everyone asked everyone else what to do now? But soon Trevor and his friends had put up long trestle tables. On went the tablecloths and the plates and plates of food, macs were hung in the cloakroom, bikes were leaning in the porch, the Brownies helped to put chairs round the tables. To be sure there was a tremendous noise, but quicker than you would believe possible, the hall was ready for tea.

'Well done, everybody,' said Brown Owl. 'Now will you sit down in the nearest chair wherever you happen to be?' As everyone was thoroughly muddled up, this meant that Gang members sat between mothers and Brownies, little children were next to big.

Tracey was sorry not to be sitting near any of her

special friends. Instead she found herself beside a big boy called Tom from Trevor's Gang, and very small Mumtas. At first, after she'd started him on his tea, she could think of nothing to say to her other neighbour. At last she thought of, 'I thought you were very clever at skating backwards.'

'Thanks,' said Tom. 'Practice, that's all.'

'You must have practised for a long time,' said Tracey politely.

'Not really. Only had the skates at Christmas. But they're a good pair and —' Once he started talking there was no stopping him. Tracey was able to eat a big tea between saying things like: 'I see,' '*Really?*' and looking after Mumtas.

Rosemary was between a mother and the youngest Brownie, so she had a relaxed tea. So did Jane, next to Farida.

'Lovely times you Brownies have,' Farida said enviously.

Jane laughed. 'It's not all playing in the park and Easter parties, you know. We work very hard sometimes.'

'What sort of work?' Farida wanted to know. Sc

Jane was kept busy throughout the meal describing Brownie life.

'Now I want to belong more than ever,' said Farida. 'And so do quite a few others from the flats, I know.'

'Fine. More the merrier,' said Jane.

'But surely you must have a limit to how many people can join?'

'In each Pack, yes, but don't forget that people keep growing out of being Brownies and become Guides, so that there are spaces. Anyway if enough people want to be Brownies in one district, and if you can find a Brown Owl to run it for you, you can start a new Pack.'

'Have you ever known that to happen?'

'Oh yes, quite recently.' Jane described how, through Tracey's accident, a Pack had been formed inside the hospital. Farida was most interested. Time flew by.

The person who was most panic-stricken was poor Susan, for after the big scraping of chairs as everyone sat down, she found herself to her horror, next to Trevor himself. At first she looked round wildly to see if she could find another place. Then she realised that manners as well as overcrowding, made that impossible. Somehow she had to get through tea. The Brownie on Trevor's other side was a new one, and not much help, so she had to manage by herself.

For some time neither she nor Trevor said anything at all, but concentrated on eating. Then Trevor suddenly asked, 'What's your brother Bill doing now then?'

Susan jumped. Of all the people she didn't want to talk about! But she had to answer something. Trying to swallow a large mouthful of doughnut she said, 'He's fine, thanks.'

'But what's he *doing*? I know he went off us after – after that bit of bother —'

'Talking of that,' said Susan, swallowing the last of her doughnut with an effort, and determined to ask the question however frightened she was (after all she'd never have a better chance) 'Have you had any more – er – bother?'

'No,' said Trevor.

'Oh, good.'

'Why, what's it to you?'

'Well, I – you —' Susan floundered, 'it wasn't a good idea was it?'

'No,' Trevor agreed. And added. 'But it was a bit of fun.'

'Fun?'

'Seemed like it at the time. Not after.'

'I should think not!'

'But you've got to do *something*,' Trevor said.

Susan thought quickly. 'I do agree. That's one of the reasons we're Brownies. Because even when we're not at meetings, or doing something special like today, we're working away at something. Too busy to be bored.'

'What sort of things?'

'Well – I don't suppose you'd really want to hear about what *we* do, it'd sound a bit babyish to someone as old as you.'

Trevor looked pleased, as Susan had hoped he would. She went on cunningly, 'The kind of thing that would interest you more would be rock-climbing or swimming or canoeing.'

'Cor, that sounds something like!' said Trevor. 'But a bit tough on girls though.'

'They'd probably prefer hikes, or learning brass-rubbing or exploring new places.'

Trevor reached for a slice of cake – then remembered to pass the plate to Susan. 'That sounds all very well, but these things aren't just laid on, you know.'

Susan gathered her courage, 'Oh but they are.'

'Yeah?'

'Honestly. In the Scouts or Guides.'

'Oh them!' said Trevor in a scornful voice. He seemed to be thinking, all the same. Susan went on eating, pretending not to be interested in Trevor.

'I thought they only went in for wearing uniforms and being goody-goody,' he said at last.

'Not a bit. Just ask Bill.' She hoped her brother wouldn't think she was letting him down in any way by discussing him. 'He really *knows*. At the moment he's busy learning the guitar to be part of a Scout folk-singing group.'

Trevor looked astonished. 'Your Bill? You're kidding!'

Then he seemed thoughtful, and not inclined to talk. Susan turned to her other neighbour. She'd said enough. She was still amazed to feel she'd spoken to the Gang's leader at all.

As the plates emptied, the noise rose. There came a moment when people began to feel they could not eat another mouthful or drink another sip, or speak another word. Brown Owl stood up, and clapped her hands for silence, and announced that this was the end of the party. One of the mothers then stood up and thanked her for all the work she'd done. Everyone clapped. Brown Owl said Nonsense, *everyone* had helped and she was grateful for all that the mothers and the Brownies had done not only today but throughout the holidays. The children from the flats clapped. Just as it seemed there were no more speeches to be made, Farida stood up, looking very fussed but determined, to say what had been planned, which was a big Thank You from everyone, children and mothers, from the flats, for everything. She stopped rather abruptly and sat down with great suddenness, but she got the biggest clap of all.

Then, after some rather sad goodbyes to the Belleview Mansions visitors, and many promises to meet again, some of the mothers took them home. Others cleared the remains of tea. Most of the plates and mugs were the throw-away kind so only the china ones they'd had to borrow from the hall, owing to unexpectedly large numbers, had to be put in the little kitchen. The Gang helped the Brownies make the room tidy and said goodbye and thank you politely to Brown Owl before they left.

Some of the younger Brownies had already gone home with their mothers, and Brown Owl suggested that everyone should follow suit except Sixers and Seconds who would help to do the little bit of washing up which was left.

It was very peaceful after they had all gone. The people left behind felt pleasantly full and tired. The sun came out after the April shower and shone through the dirty windows.

'But it didn't matter that it rained,' Rosemary said. 'We'd had the important outdoor bit already.'

The others agreed. The Party had been a great success.

'And your scones were delicious, Tracey,' said Brown Owl.

Tracey had a horribly difficult moment. It would

have been so easy just to say 'Thank you' and leave it at that. Yet somehow that would have spoilt the whole day. She knew she mustn't miss the chance to put this right. She went very red as she mumbled indistinctly, but somehow, clutching her tea-towel in damp fingers, she managed to get out: 'Actually, I didn't make them. Mum did.'

Everybody realised how hard it had been for Tracey to say that in front of them, Brown Owl as much as anyone.

'Well done, Tracey,' she said. 'I knew you'd tell us. Your mother told me the whole story during tea.'

Oh how glad Tracey was that she'd told the truth! Supposing she hadn't? She felt hotter than ever at the thought. But the others were clamouring: 'What story?' so she described her own disastrous efforts and made the tale so funny that she ended up laughing with the rest, instead of crying. In the middle of the uproar a clearing of the throat was heard in the kitchen doorway.

There stood Trevor. He caught Brown Owl's eye as the laughing died away.

'Er – just come to see if I could give you a hand?' he suggested, looking thoroughly embarrassed.

'How kind,' said Brown Owl. 'I wonder if you'd like to sweep the hall for us? It needs it badly. I'll come and show you where the brushes are kept.'

It was while they were both rummaging in a half-darkness of the broom cupboard that Trevor blurted out, 'I wanted to ask you something – of course I don't mind helping as well, but, it was something that young Susan was saying at tea-time. I wondered if you could tell us – me – a bit more . . .' At last he got it out. He and his Gang were getting pretty sick of making nuisances of themselves. Was there anything worth while in the Scouting business? Or the Guides?

'Certainly there is,' said Brown Owl. 'And there I *can* help you!' (Though she privately thought that Susan had done the best of the work already.) 'I know the people concerned. No need to decide anything in a hurry of course . . .'

Which is how it came to be that when the hall was spick and span and locked, the Brownies who had been looking forward to walking home with Brown Owl and talking over the party were told: 'You've done a very good day's work. You won't mind taking yourselves home will you? Trevor and I have an errand to do in another direction. Thank you again so much. Good night!'

'Good night!' chorused the Brownies.

But as Trevor went off talking earnestly to Brown Owl, Tracey said, 'She's UP to something. You can always tell.'

'Fancy, her and Trevor,' said Jane.

'He won't be an enemy any more, anyway,' said Rosemary thankfully. 'Goodness. I'm tired.'

'Me too,' said everyone.

Jane yawned. Everyone found herself yawning as well. They set off together, people breaking off their different ways till only Jane and Tracey were left.

'I say,' Tracey said awkwardly. 'I've been a bit beastly. I didn't mean to. I'm sorry.'

'Is it Susan, or me being a Sixer?' Jane asked, not pretending she didn't understand.

'Both. Neither. I don't know. Just me being silly, I think.'

'So do I,' said Jane comfortably. 'Anyway don't let's talk about it. It's not important.'

'Not any more,' Tracey agreed, suddenly finding this was true.

'Come in for a quick word with Mum before you go home?'

'Thanks, I'd like to.'

The two friends turned in at Jane's gate together.

Other Brownie titles:

THE BROWNIES IN HOSPITAL *by Pamela Sykes*
THE SECRET BROWNIES *by Dorothy Richardson*
THE BROWNIE VENTURERS *by Dorothy Richardson*
THE BROWNIE ELEPHANT HUNTERS *by Dorothy Richardson*
THE BROWNIE CAMPAIGNERS *by Dorothy Richardson*